GROUNDBREAKING WOMEN IN POLITICS

ILHAN OMAR

by Jeanne Marie Ford

FOCUS
READERS.

VOYAGER

www.focusreaders.com

Focus Readers is distributed by North Star Editions:
sales@northstareditions.com | 888-417-0195

Produced for Focus Readers by Red Line Editorial.

Content Consultant: Christina Bejarano, Professor of Multicultural Women's and Gender Studies, Texas Woman's University

Photographs ©: Alex Edelman/picture-alliance/dpa/AP Images, cover, 1; Susan Walsh/AP Images, 4–5; Glen Stubbe/Star Tribune/AP Images, 7; mustafa olgun/Shutterstock Images, 8–9; Sadik Gulec/Shutterstock Images, 11; Karthikeyan Rajendran/Shutterstock Images, 13; benedek/iStockphoto, 14–15; David Joles/Zuma Press/Newscom, 17; Aaron Lavinsky/Star Tribune/AP Images, 19; Jacob Boomsma/Shutterstock Images, 20–21; Rawpixel.com/Shutterstock Images, 23; Carlos Gonzalez/Zuma Press/Newscom, 25; Action Sports Photography/Shutterstock Images, 26–27; Glen Stubbe/Zuma Press/Newscom, 29, 34–35; Rachael Warriner/Shutterstock Images, 31; Red Line Editorial, 33, 39; Mark Vancleave/Minneapolis Star Tribune/TNS/Newscom, 37; Eli Wilson/Shutterstock Images, 40–41; Saeschie Wagner/Shutterstock Images, 43; J. Scott Applewhite/AP Images, 45

Library of Congress Cataloging-in-Publication Data
Names: Ford, Jeanne Marie, 1971- author.
Title: Ilhan Omar / by Jeanne Marie Ford.
Description: Lake Elmo, MN : Focus Readers, [2020] | Series: Groundbreaking
   women in politics | Includes index. | Audience: Grades 4-6
Identifiers: LCCN 2019036408 (print) | LCCN 2019036409 (ebook) | ISBN
   9781644930908 (hardcover) | ISBN 9781644931691 (paperback) | ISBN
   9781644933275 (pdf) | ISBN 9781644932483 (ebook)
Subjects: LCSH: Omar, Ilhan, 1982---Juvenile literature. | Women
   legislators--United States--Biography--Juvenile literature. |
   Legislators--United States--Biography--Juvenile literature. | United
   States. Congress. House--Biography--Juvenile literature.
Classification: LCC E901.1.O43 F67 2020 (print) | LCC E901.1.O43 (ebook) |
   DDC 328.73/092 [B]--dc23
LC record available at https://lccn.loc.gov/2019036408
LC ebook record available at https://lccn.loc.gov/2019036409

Printed in the United States of America
Mankato, MN
012020

ABOUT THE AUTHOR

Jeanne Marie Ford is an Emmy-winning TV scriptwriter who holds a Master of Fine Arts degree in writing for children from Vermont College. She has written numerous children's books and articles. Ford also teaches college English. She lives in Maryland with her husband and two children.

TABLE OF CONTENTS

CHAPTER 1

SWEARING IN

On January 3, 2019, Ilhan Omar was sworn in to the US House of Representatives. For the ceremony, she laid her hand on a red Quran. The book had belonged to her late grandfather, Abukar. He had inspired Omar on the journey that brought her to this new role. She wished he could be there to see this moment.

Omar's father, Nur, stood next to her as she raised her right hand. He had tears in his eyes.

Ilhan Omar stands with her father and Speaker Nancy Pelosi during the swearing-in ceremony.

Later that day, Omar stood with her six-year-old daughter, Ilwad, on the House floor. A guest told Ilwad that someday she might be in Congress, too. Ilwad said no. She said she would be president.

More than 20 years earlier, Omar first set foot in Washington, DC. She had come with her family from a **refugee** camp in Kenya. Now, she had returned to Washington to become the first Somali American member of Congress.

In more ways than one, this 116th Congress was more diverse than ever before. A record 102 women were serving in the House of Representatives. Sharice Davids and Deb Haaland were Congress's first two American Indian women. And Omar was one of the first two Muslim women in Congress. Rashida Tlaib was the other.

Omar looked forward to working with the other members of Congress, new and old. For example,

Omar's daughter, Ilwad, rests her chin on her mother's shoulder in the House chamber.

she had looked up to Representative John Lewis for many years. This civil rights leader had served in Congress for more than 30 years. Now, Omar, Lewis, and others would be working together to help the people of the United States.

CHAPTER 2

EARLY LIFE

Ilhan Omar was born on October 4, 1982, in Mogadishu, Somalia. She was raised in the town of Baidoa, a few hours northwest of Mogadishu. When Ilhan was a little girl, her grandfather told her the same folktale every day. It was about a Somali queen named Araweelo. The women in Araweelo's kingdom were rulers. The men were their subjects. Araweelo was wise and just. Ilhan hoped to be like her someday.

Much of Somalia, including Baidoa, is in a desert climate.

Ilhan was the youngest of seven children. When she was only two years old, her mother died. After that, Ilhan was raised by her grandfather and her father. They taught Ilhan to say what was on her mind. They made her feel special.

Many of Ilhan's relatives were teachers. After school, she came home and continued her studies with them. The large extended family ate lunch together. They listened to the radio and talked about news and politics. Life was good.

But when Ilhan was eight years old, a civil war started in Somalia. One night, soldiers arrived outside her family's home. A silence fell over the home. She heard the men talking about how they would force their way in. They tried to break down the door. Then came the sound of bullets.

Ilhan hid under her bed with her sister and her aunt. The next morning, the soldiers were gone,

As of 2019, more than 250,000 Somali people were staying in Kenyan refugee camps.

but marks from their bullets remained in the walls. Ilhan's family decided their home was no longer safe. Neighbors were fighting against neighbors. They needed to leave Somalia.

Ilhan's grandfather knew people in the neighboring country of Kenya who could help them. Ilhan's family settled in a refugee camp at the edge of the jungle near Mombasa, Kenya.

Ilhan wandered around the tents and huts of the camp. To her, it felt like a playground.

In Somalia, Ilhan's family had been wealthy. They had servants, and their home was filled with books. But in the refugee camp, their family had no access to running water or toilets. Waiting for an outhouse could take hours. Ilhan carried water and did other chores for her family.

After four years in the camp, a church helped Ilhan's family move to Arlington, Virginia, in the United States. Ilhan was excited but nervous. She knew only a few words of English.

The US government sent videos so the family could learn about life in the United States. Everything looked beautiful to 12-year-old Ilhan. The videos showed green lawns, nice houses, and grocery stores filled with food. But when their plane landed in New York City, the landscape

New York City has the highest population of any city in the United States.

looked very different from what she had expected. Car horns blared. She saw walls covered by graffiti and people begging on the streets.

Ilhan turned to her father in shock. This looked different from the America her father had promised. He told her to be patient. They had not yet reached their new home.

CHAPTER 3

A NEW HOME

Ilhan Omar had always lived among people who had certain things in common. Everyone she had known in Somalia and Kenya was black and Muslim. But at her new school in Virginia, most students were white. Few were Muslim.

At lunch, Ilhan sat alone. The cafeteria workers were kind, but other students stared at her. They stuck gum to her hijab. They made fun of her when she changed in the locker room.

When Ilhan came to Arlington in 1995, fewer than 3 percent of people there had been born in Africa.

Ilhan asked her father for advice. He said Ilhan was not being teased because other students disliked her. Rather, these students felt threatened by her because she was different. He encouraged Ilhan to learn English quickly. This way, she could talk to her new classmates. It was hard for people to hate others from up close, he said.

As soon as Ilhan learned enough English, the other kids peppered her with rude questions. They asked if she had a pet monkey. They asked what it felt like to wear shoes for the first time. They asked if she had hair under her hijab.

Ilhan's family wanted to feel more accepted. In 1997, they moved to the Cedar-Riverside neighborhood of Minneapolis, Minnesota. This neighborhood had the largest community of Somali Americans in the United States. In Minneapolis, the family began to make another

△ Cedar-Riverside has been home to thousands of Somali people since the civil war in Somalia started in 1991.

new life for themselves. Ilhan's grandfather also became involved in local politics. That year, he asked 14-year-old Ilhan to come to a Democratic Party **caucus**.

This party is one of two major US political parties. Democrats often push for liberal changes. Socially, they also support greater freedoms. The Republican Party is the other major party.

Republicans usually take **conservative** stances. They favor maintaining traditional social values.

Ilhan's grandfather needed her to translate for him at the caucus. She helped her grandfather vote for candidates. She felt involved in something bigger than herself. That day sparked Ilhan's interest in politics.

Ilhan also formed a diversity and unity club at her high school. She had seen conflicts between classmates of different races and cultures. Students in the club learned that they had a lot in common. They learned those things mattered more than their differences.

> ## ➤ THINK ABOUT IT

Do you agree with Ilhan's father that it's harder to feel hatred toward a group of people once you know individuals from that group? Why or why not?

Voters participate in a Democratic Party caucus in Minneapolis.

On September 11, 2001, terrorists attacked the United States, killing nearly 3,000 people. The terrorists were part of an Islamic militant group. After the attacks, **Islamophobia** rose sharply in the United States. In response, Ilhan decided to wear the hijab. She wanted to show her fellow citizens she was proud to be Muslim.

CHAPTER 4

ENTERING POLITICS

After high school, Ilhan Omar attended North Dakota State University. She majored in political science and international studies. During college, Omar began to see what she wanted her life's work to be. She hoped to build bridges between people of different backgrounds and beliefs. For this reason, Omar volunteered at Democratic meetings. She also organized the university's first Islamic awareness week.

North Dakota State University is located in the city of Fargo, North Dakota.

After college, Omar moved back to Minneapolis. She worked for the University of Minnesota. She taught families and children about nutrition.

In 2013, Andrew Johnson hired Omar to be his campaign manager. Johnson was running for Minneapolis City Council. City councils make laws at the city level. When Johnson won the election, he made Omar one of his top aides. Omar helped Johnson with policy research. She also met with people living in Johnson's **district**. She told Johnson which issues mattered to those people.

For example, most restaurants and cafés in Minneapolis were not allowed to stay open past 11:00 p.m. During the month-long holiday of Ramadan, however, Muslims do not eat during the day. As a result, many businesses in Muslim communities were losing money during the holiday. In response, Omar worked with Johnson

to change the law. This change let businesses stay open later during Ramadan.

In 2014, Omar watched the race for District 60B in the Minnesota House. Omar had grown up in the district. Phyllis Kahn had represented it for more than 40 years. That year, Somali American Mohamud Noor was running against her. Kahn won, but Noor planned to run again in 2016.

However, Omar felt she would also make a good candidate. She thought she could make sure Somali voices were heard at the state level.

She also thought she could build connections between the district's many communities. In 2015, Omar entered the race for District 60B.

Omar knew the **primary** election would be tough. Kahn held a lot of influence. And with Noor in the race, Omar faced challenges from within the Somali community, too. Many held traditional beliefs about the role of women in society. Some women told Omar they wanted to vote for her, but their husbands would not let them.

Despite these obstacles, Omar ran a strong campaign. She worked to overcome resistance in

> THINK ABOUT IT

People outside the Muslim community might not have easily understood how Ramadan could affect certain businesses. Are there issues in your community that other people might not understand?

▲ Omar and her supporters celebrate after winning her 2016 election.

the Somali community. She also met with groups of the district's many college students. And she engaged people who had not voted before. Omar's efforts paid off. On August 9, 2016, voter turnout in her district increased by 37 percent. Omar won with approximately 41 percent of the vote.

The primary was the hard part. District 60B was heavily Democratic. On November 8, 2016, Omar received nearly 81 percent of the vote in the general election. She became the first elected Somali American lawmaker in the nation.

CHAPTER 5

RISING STAR

For most Democrats, the excitement of Omar's win was overshadowed by the national election results. Donald Trump had won the presidential race. During his campaign, Trump had said he wanted to ban all Muslims from entering the United States. Trump had also described Somali refugees as a disaster for the state of Minnesota.

Omar addressed these attitudes in public. In July 2017, Omar appeared on a national talk show.

Presidential candidate Donald Trump speaks at a rally in February 2016.

She invited President Trump to Somali tea. She said he could learn about her community in person. She said that might be helpful for him. Trump did not accept the invitation.

Omar's fame and influence continued to rise in the following months. She appeared on the cover of a popular magazine. A movie about her 2016 campaign came out. Omar even inspired a hijab-wearing doll. Not all the attention she received was positive, however. Omar received a great deal of criticism. Critics questioned some of her personal relationships. Others wanted to start investigations into Omar's use of campaign funds.

Omar did not let the spotlight distract from her work. While in office, she served on three different committees. These committees focused on education, government data, and state finance. Omar helped bring a large amount of state

▲ Omar speaks against a proposed bill during a May 2018 session of the Minnesota House.

funding to her district as well. She believed this money would help create jobs.

Omar also introduced a number of **bills** to the House. These bills did not become law during her time in state office. But they showed which issues Omar cared about most. Some bills would have provided funding to communities of color, especially women of color. Others would have increased protections for immigrants and refugees.

For example, Omar tried to change Minnesota's relationship with Immigration and Customs Enforcement (ICE). This agency enforces US immigration laws. As part of this role, ICE detains undocumented immigrants. ICE also deports, or removes, many of these people from the country. ICE often works with local law enforcement to perform this job.

However, numerous immigrants have reported abuse from ICE agents. Omar believes ICE should not be holding most of these immigrants in the first place. In fact, Omar believes ICE should no longer exist. As a result, one of Omar's bills tried

➤ THINK ABOUT IT

Few state-level politicians become nationally known. Why do you think Ilhan Omar attracted so much attention?

△ Protesters march in support of immigrants in Philadelphia, Pennsylvania.

to make Minnesota a sanctuary state. This type of state chooses not to work with ICE.

By June 2018, Omar was nearing the end of her first term. That month, Keith Ellison announced he was not running for reelection in the US House of Representatives. Ellison had represented Minnesota's Fifth District for years. Omar decided she wanted to serve Minnesotans at the national level. Omar entered the race to fill his seat.

IMMIGRATION

In January 2017, President Trump signed an order to reject immigrants from many majority-Muslim countries. Ilhan Omar was among a number of congressional Democrats who opposed the order. In April 2019, they introduced the No Ban Act to counter this order.

Trump's order had twice been ruled unconstitutional in court. Each time, Trump signed a new, rewritten order. The US Supreme Court upheld the third version in June 2018. As a result, nearly 40,000 people were prevented from traveling to the United States that year. Many families were separated. People with serious illnesses could no longer travel to get medical care in the United States.

The issue of immigration was personal to Omar. Her daughter, Ilwad, saw President Trump on TV. He was talking about restricting the entry

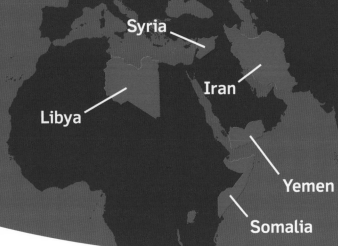

President Trump's Travel Ban

Syria

Iran

Libya

Yemen

Somalia

Five majority-Muslim countries were affected by the US travel ban upheld by the Supreme Court in 2018.

of Muslims into the United States. Ilwad turned off the TV. She said if the president didn't want them in his home, she didn't want him in hers.

In a tweet in support of the No Ban Act, Omar wrote that no one should lose access to basic rights because of religion, race, or place of birth. Omar said she had always believed in the American dream of liberty and justice for all. But to Omar, Trump's policies threatened that dream.

The Republican-controlled Senate was unlikely to pass the No Ban Act. But Omar and her fellow Democrats vowed that they would continue to fight for immigrants' rights.

CHAPTER 6

MAKING HISTORY

Five other Democratic candidates ran against Ilhan Omar for Minnesota's Fifth District seat. Margaret Anderson Kelliher was one of these candidates. Anderson Kelliher had been Minnesota's House Speaker for several years. Patricia Torres Ray was another candidate. Torres Ray had served in the state senate for 12 years. Torres Ray and Anderson Kelliher campaigned on their experience to appeal to voters.

Omar speaks at a 2018 debate with Patricia Torres Ray (left) and Margaret Anderson Kelliher.

Omar did not have much experience as a lawmaker. Instead, her campaign focused on other priorities. Similar to 2016, Omar worked to get a lot of new people to vote. She also made sure her campaign team was young and diverse.

Omar ran on **progressive** issues. For example, she wanted to get rid of college students' debt. She wanted to ban private prisons. She also wanted to increase the number of refugees legally admitted to the United States.

In August 2018, Omar won the Democratic primary. She got nearly 20 percent more votes than Anderson Kelliher, the runner-up. After that win, Omar was almost certain to take the Fifth District seat in the general election. Like District 60B, this district was home to many Democrats. Republicans rarely received more than 25 percent of the vote.

▲ Omar gives a victory speech after winning her 2018 election.

Indeed, on November 6, 2018, Omar won 78 percent of the vote. She was headed to Washington, DC. That night, Omar and her supporters celebrated her win. People of all cultures, races, and ages filled the room.

ECONOMIC JUSTICE

Throughout her career, Ilhan Omar has pushed for economic justice. This idea means all people should have the opportunity to do meaningful, well-paid work. Omar believes the United States does not provide these opportunities to everyone.

For example, the top 1 percent of earners control nearly 40 percent of US wealth. On average, women earn only 81 percent as much as men for the same work. And more than 40 percent of US workers earn less than $15 per hour. The average one-bedroom apartment requires an income of nearly $18 per hour.

Economic justice also matters a lot to Omar's own district. In 2018, the Fifth District had a large low-income population. It also had the state's highest unemployment rate.

Omar supported a number of solutions to these problems. She wanted to raise Minneapolis's

US Wage Gaps, 2018

When both race and gender are factored in, US wage gaps are often greater than when only gender is factored in.

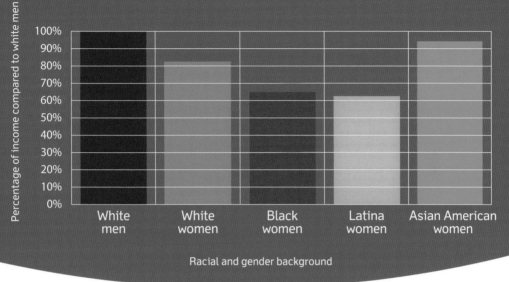

Percentage of income compared to white men

Racial and gender background

minimum wage to $15 per hour. She believed the US government should do the same across the country. In 2019, the US minimum wage had been $7.25 per hour for 10 years.

In addition, Omar supported a program known as a jobs guarantee. This program would make sure everyone who wanted a job would have one. These jobs would pay at least $15 per hour. Omar believed these changes would push the United States closer to economic justice.

CHAPTER 7

LOOKING AHEAD

For 181 years, Congress had banned headwear from its chambers. But for Ilhan Omar, wearing a hijab was about her religious freedom. In January 2019, Omar and other House Democrats changed the rule. Omar became the first member of Congress to wear a hijab on the House floor.

Not everyone was happy about this moment. A conservative pastor said that Congress would soon look similar to an Islamic republic.

Omar speaks in front of the US Capitol in 2019.

In response, Omar tweeted that Congress was going to look like America. People like the pastor would just have to get used to it.

However, these sensitive religious issues kept following Omar. In February, Republican Kevin McCarthy shared one of Omar's old tweets, which criticized Israel. Israel has controlled parts of Palestine for decades. Omar and many others believe Israel is wrongfully harming Palestinians.

However, the United States is one of Israel's strongest allies. McCarthy wanted Democrats to punish Omar for her statements. In response, Omar tweeted that a pro-Israel political group was helping fund many US politicians. She suggested that these politicians support Israel in exchange for this money.

Leaders of Omar's own party condemned this tweet. They said it played into **anti-Semitic** ideas

▲ In 2002, Israel began building a 400-mile (640-km) wall to separate Israel from Palestine.

about Jewish people. One of these false ideas is that Jewish people control the world through money. Omar apologized. People helped her understand the painful history of anti-Semitism.

But the next month, Omar made more comments that many viewed as anti-Semitic. This time, Omar did not apologize. She said she was criticizing political groups and Israel's government, not Jewish people. But not everyone agreed on the line between the two.

As a result, many people in her district were unhappy. In 2019, more than half of Minnesota's Jewish residents lived in Omar's district. Some felt betrayed by her remarks. However, others felt Omar was being targeted only because she was Muslim. Many women in Congress, especially women of color, came to Omar's defense.

House Democratic leaders tried to pass a **resolution** against anti-Semitism. However, the version that passed condemned many forms of hate speech. This kind of speech can include both anti-Semitism and Islamophobia. Omar noted it was the first time Congress had ever come out against Islamophobia.

President Trump and other conservatives continued to target Omar. But she did her best to focus on her work. In June 2019, she put forward a bill about student lunch debt. Many low-income

In July 2019, Omar and three other congresswomen condemned Trump's recent comments about them.

students are unable to pay for school meals. Some schools make these students' names public. Omar's bill would stop schools from shaming students who cannot afford lunch.

This bill showed Omar's commitment to progressive values. Her success also created new possibilities for immigrants, Muslims, and women of color. To many, Omar represented the best of a new generation in politics.

FOCUS ON
ILHAN OMAR

Write your answers on a separate piece of paper.

1. Write a paragraph describing the main ideas of Chapter 5.

2. Do you think Ilhan Omar's proposed economic policies would be good for the country? Why or why not?

3. When was Omar elected to the US House of Representatives?

   A. 2013
   B. 2016
   C. 2018

4. Why might Omar's support for a jobs guarantee be in line with the Democratic Party's values?

   A. Democrats tend to support an active government role in the economy.
   B. Democrats tend to take conservative stances.
   C. Democrats tend to support fewer social freedoms.

Answer key on page 48.

GLOSSARY

anti-Semitic
Having to do with hatred of or prejudice against Jewish people.

bills
Written plans to create or change laws.

caucus
A meeting of party members to select that party's candidate for a general election.

conservative
Supporting traditional views or values, often resisting changes.

district
An area that votes to elect a representative.

Islamophobia
Hatred of, fear of, or prejudice against Muslim people.

primary
An election that decides a political party's nominee for a general election.

progressive
In favor of making changes or improvements away from traditional norms, especially relating to political or social issues.

refugee
A person forced to leave his or her home due to war or other dangers.

resolution
A government body's official statement of position on an issue or event.

TO LEARN MORE

BOOKS

Gunderson, Jessica. *Immigrants from Somalia and Other African Countries*. North Mankato, MN: Capstone Press, 2019.

Hassig, Susan M., et al. *Somalia*. New York: Cavendish Square Publishing, 2017.

Staley, Erin. *The Most Influential Female Activists*. New York: Rosen Publishing, 2019.

NOTE TO EDUCATORS

Visit **www.focusreaders.com** to find lesson plans, activities, links, and other resources related to this title.

INDEX

Answer Key: 1. Answers will vary; **2.** Answers will vary; **3.** C; **4.** A